IS IT TRU

1
......

1. JESUS—the Man of history

Jesus is a historical person who can be our Saviour and real Friend today

Let's be clear: Jesus Christ really existed. He is not a mythical figure or a nice guy in some fairy tale. Nor is he an imaginary friend we turn to for comfort when we walk through those terrifying experiences of life. He was born, lived, died, rose again, returned to heaven, and is coming back one day.

Testimonies from history that Jesus lived

- Tacitus, the Roman historian who lived around twenty years after Jesus, refers to Jesus as having been executed by Pontius Pilate, the governor of Judea, during the reign of the Roman emperor Tiberius.

- A Jewish historian called Josephus, born four years after Jesus' crucifixion, referred to Jesus as a real person in history and records the death of 'James the brother of Jesus'.

- Serapion, a Syrian philosopher, who lived not long after Jesus, refers to Jesus in his writings as a real person in history.

- Around AD 178, a Roman philosopher, Celsus, who was dead-set against Christianity, refers to Jesus as a historical person who really lived.

Today, the idea that Jesus Christ is a myth finds virtually no support from scholars of the Bible or history.

To pretend Jesus never lived is like claiming the moon is made of green cheese!

Eyewitnesses of Jesus

The writers of the New Testament Gospels—Matthew, Mark, Luke and John— give the history of Jesus' teaching and ministry.

- Luke researched carefully to uncover the facts. *'Since I myself have carefully investigated everything from the beginning, it seemed good also to me to write an orderly account for you … so that you may know the certainty of the things you have been taught'* (Luke 1:1–4).

- At the end of his Gospel, John, a close disciple of Jesus, promised his readers: *'This is the disciple who testifies to these things … we know that his testimony is true'* (John 21:24).

- Peter, another disciple wrote, *'… We did not follow cleverly invented stories when we told you about the power and coming of our Lord Jesus Christ, but we were eye-witnesses of his majesty'* (2 Peter 1:16–18).

The question is not 'Did Jesus really live?' but, 'Who was he?'

Tacitus is considered by scholars to be a reliable historian of the Roman emperors

2. JESUS—his identity

Who is Jesus Christ? This is the most important question you can ever ask

People have not been able to airbrush Jesus out of history. They keep asking 'Who is he?' There have been several ideas:

A good man?
A religious teacher?
A prophet?
A con-man?
A mad man?

Even when Jesus walked this earth people asked this question, especially after the astonishing events in his life.

- Jesus had been working some miracles in Galilee and the news reached the palace of the King. Puzzled, Herod couldn't work it out, and asked, *'**Who is this** I hear such things about?'* (Luke 9:9).

- On Palm Sunday, *'When Jesus entered Jerusalem, the whole city was stirred and asked, "**Who is this?**"'* (Matthew 21:10).

- On one occasion an event took place that was both terrifying and wonderful. Matthew gives us a dramatic eyewitness account:

  'Without warning, a furious storm came up on the lake, so that the waves swept over the boat. But Jesus was sleeping. The disciples went and woke him, saying, "Lord, save us! We're going to drown!" He replied, "You of little faith, why are you so afraid?" Then he

It would have been a small Galilean fishing boat like this from which Jesus stilled the storm

got up and rebuked the winds and the waves, and it was completely calm. The men were amazed and asked, **"What kind of man is this?** *Even the winds and the waves obey him!"* (Matthew 8:23–27).

- When an immoral woman fell at Jesus feet, crying bitterly for she was so sorry for her sins, Jesus said that he forgave her. This seemed an outrageous, even blasphemous, thing to do, and *'The other guests began to say among themselves,* **"Who is this** *who even forgives sins?"'* (Luke 7:49).

The question of who Jesus really is became a national talking point. One day he asked his own disciples who they thought he was: *'But what about you?* **Who do you say I am?***'* They gave various answers and finally, Simon Peter replied with a history-shaking statement: *'The Christ [Messiah] of God'* (Luke 9:20).

Right now, **Who do you say Jesus is?** To uncover the truth, we need to go back to the historically reliable writings in the Bible and answer this question that determines our eternity: **'Who is Jesus?'**

3. JESUS—
the long-expected Messiah

Everything Jesus came to do had been planned for a long time

When God created the human race, Adam and Eve rebelled against him (Genesis 3) and this beautiful, orderly world turned into an ugly mess. Every relationship that God had established was ripped apart. People turned against God and terrible human tragedies began.

All through the Old Testament (the Scriptures of the Jews), God made promises that one day he would send a Rescuer who would release those imprisoned by dark powers and would speak and act on behalf of downtrodden and sinful people. In ancient Israel he was known as the '**Messiah**' (a word that means 'anointed'), and the earliest prophecies in the Bible foretold what wonderful things he would do. Here are a few of many:

Prophecies of the Messiah

- '*In your majesty ride forth victoriously on behalf of truth, humility and righteousness; let your right-hand display awesome deeds*' (Psalm 45:4).

- '*The Spirit of the Sovereign LORD is on me, because the LORD has anointed me to preach good news to the poor. He has sent me to bind up the broken-hearted, to proclaim freedom for the captives and release from darkness for the prisoners, to proclaim the year of the LORD's favour...*' (Isaiah 61:1,2) .

- *'He was pierced for our transgressions, he was crushed for our iniquities; the punishment that brought us peace was upon him, and by his wounds we are healed. We all, like sheep, have gone astray, each of us has turned to his own way, and the LORD has laid on him the iniquity of us all.'* (Isaiah 53:5,6).

Imagine the anticipation for this Mighty Saviour. One who would defend truth, promote humility, bring justice, comfort the brokenhearted, rebuild destroyed lives, offer forgiveness and announce peace to those in rebellion against God. People were longing for this Messiah.

Enter Jesus the Messiah

One day Jesus was talking to a woman by a well in Samaria whose life was sinful and broken. She needed to be rescued, restored and forgiven. She expressed her longing: *'I know that Messiah is coming. When he comes, he will explain everything to us.'* Jesus replied, *'I, who speak to you am he'* (John 4:25,26). This was one of the most significant moments of history—Jesus claiming that he is the Messiah.

A true new age had dawned. Jesus had come from heaven to restore people to God, to creation, to themselves and to others.

Life can begin again.

4. JESUS—
the birth of the Messiah

The miraculous birth of this baby reveals who he is and brings hope for every person

At a town called Nazareth in Israel, an angel from God appeared to a young virgin girl named Mary and told her: *'The Holy Spirit will come upon you, and the power of the Most High will overshadow you. So the holy one to be born will be called the Son of God'* (Luke 1:35).

Mary miraculously conceived a baby without any sexual activity. There was a special reason for this as we will see. Why should it be impossible with God?

Mary was engaged to be married to Joseph who, when he found out Mary was pregnant, thought the worst. But an angel told Joseph: *'Do not be afraid to take Mary home as your wife, because what is conceived in her is from the Holy Spirit. She will give birth to a son, and you are to give him the name Jesus because he will save his people from their sins'* (Matthew 1:20,21).

When the baby was born in Bethlehem, there were some shepherds, working-class guys, protecting their flocks. An angel appeared and told them: *'I bring you good news of great joy that will be for all the people. Today in the town of David a Saviour has been born to you; he is the Christ [Messiah] the Lord.'* Suddenly a crowd of angels proclaimed, *'Glory to God in the highest heaven, and on earth peace to those on whom his favour rests'* (Luke 2:10,14).

Sometime after his birth a few rich upper-class Wise Men, followed a star to search for Jesus. They found him and gave him gifts of gold, frankincense and myrrh. They knew who he was and so they *'bowed down and worshipped him'* (Matthew 2:11).

Why a virgin birth?

Jesus had no human father and a young virgin for his mother to make it clear that he was no ordinary child but 'the Son of God'. Some people misunderstand what that means. Because Jesus always existed and never had a beginning, 'Son of God' simply describes his relationship with God the Father. It is his title. He was with 'God the Father' and equal with him from all eternity.

Jesus' birth was good news to all kinds of people and to all nations. His birth is good news for you. He did not come just to tell us good news—Jesus **is** the Good News.

'For God so loved the world that he gave his one and only Son, that whoever believes in him shall not perish but have eternal life. For God did not send his Son into the world to condemn the world, but to save the world through him' (John 3:16)

5. JESUS—
really God and really Man

Jesus was human so that he could identify with us, but he was also God so that he was perfect to save us

This is a mystery! This goes way beyond our small minds, but the Bible is quite clear that when Jesus was here on planet earth, he was always both God and Man at the same time.

Jesus was a real Man

He was born as a real human. He had a human body (Hebrews 10:5,10,20). He needed to sleep (Mark 4:38). He became thirsty (John 4:7) and hungry (Matthew 4:2). He shed real blood (John 19:34). Jesus had human emotions: he wept (John 11:35), rejoiced (Luke 10:21), and felt sorrow (Mark 14:34).

But at the same time Jesus was truly God

Jesus did things that only God could do:

- He was all-powerful and able to control the weather (Mark 4:39).
- He could raise dead people to life (John 11:43).
- He knew exactly what people were thinking (Mark 2:8; John 2:25).
- He forgave people their sin, and the Jews agreed: *'Who can forgive sins but God alone?'* (Luke 5:21).

Jesus claimed to be God

He claimed, *'Before Abraham was born, I am!'* (John 8:58). 'I AM' was the exact name that God revealed to

Moses to describe himself (Exodus 3:14). It revealed God as eternal, without beginning or end. God is always the 'I AM'. For this claim the Jews wanted to kill Jesus (John 8:59).

Often Jesus claimed to be 'the Son of God' and that God was his 'Father'. The Jews wanted to stone him because *'He was even calling God his own Father, making himself equal with God.'* Far from denying it, Jesus immediately referred to himself as the 'Son' of God no less than seven times (John 5:16–23).

He accepted worship: *'That all may honour the Son just as they honour the Father'* (John 5:23). *'Just as'* means 'in exactly the same way.'

One of his disciples addressed Jesus as: *'My Lord and my God'* (John 20:28). Jesus did not correct or rebuke him.

Why was Jesus both God and Man?

As God he showed how much God cares for us. But as a perfect Man he never sinned and could therefore take the punishment our sin deserved.

In front of the crowds, Jesus claimed that God was his Father. The religious leaders knew he was claiming to be equal with God

6. JESUS—the Trinity

Jesus is truly God and truly Man, but there is only one God

God revealed himself to Moses: *'Hear, O Israel. The LORD our God, the LORD is one'* (Deuteronomy 6:4). There is only one God. But in Genesis 1:26 God uses the plural 'us' to refer to himself when he says *'Let us make man.'* This hints that there is a mystery in the Creator. The language of the Old Testament is Hebrew and the Hebrew word for God is *Elohim*, a plural word.

The Father is God

In the Old Testament God was often described as the 'Father' of Israel (Deuteronomy 32:6 for example). In the New Testament, the title 'Father' referred to one person in the Trinity: *'There is but one God, the Father, from whom all things came'* (1 Corinthians 8:6).

Jesus the Son is God

Look back at the previous chapter.

The New Testament describes Jesus this way: *'By him all things were created… for God was pleased to have all his fulness dwell in him'* (Colossians 1:16,19), and *'Jesus, being in very nature God'* (Philippians 2:6).

John made this clear when he referred to Jesus as 'the Word': *'In the beginning was the Word, and the Word was with God, and the Word was God'* (John 1:1). Calling Jesus 'the Word' was a way of saying that God the Father speaks to us in the life of Jesus.

Jesus is the eternal Son of the Father (John 1:14)

The Holy Spirit is God

The Holy Spirit is a person, not a 'force' or a 'power'. Jesus gave him the title 'he': *'When he, the Spirit of truth, comes, he will guide you into all truth'* (John 16:13). The New Testament refers to the Spirit as one who can teach, counsel, speak, send, convict, be blasphemed against, lied to and grieved—these can only be used of a person.

He is the 'eternal Spirit' (Hebrews 9:14), present everywhere (Psalm 139:7–10), even at creation (Genesis 1:2).

This is not three gods

Nor is it one God revealing himself in three different ways. Throughout the Bible, God is revealed as three separate Persons in one Godhead—distinct, yet undivided. A perfect 'tri-unity'. Jesus' disciples baptized new Christians: *'in the name of the Father and of the Son and of the Holy Spirit'* (Matthew 28:19).

This is a deep mystery, far beyond the limitations of language and the human mind. This should lead us to adore and worship God.

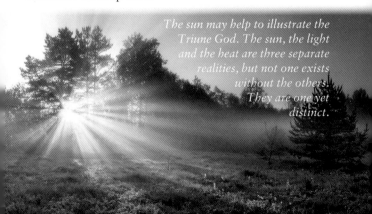

The sun may help to illustrate the Triune God. The sun, the light and the heat are three separate realities, but not one exists without the others. They are one yet distinct.

7. JESUS—his character

Jesus was the kindest, most compassionate and forgiving person the world has ever known

We don't have a portrait of Jesus, but we are told a lot about his character—the real Man.

The character of Jesus is the best ever

- Some of his critics admitted: *'Teacher, we know that you are a man of **integrity**. You aren't swayed by others, because you pay no attention to who they are'* (Mark 12:14).
- Jesus said: *'Learn from me, for I am **gentle** and **humble** in heart, and you will find rest for your souls'* (Matthew 11:29).
- *'I have spoken to you so that my **joy** may be in you...'* (John 15:11). *'My **peace** I give you'* (John 14:27).
- *'Greater **love** has no one than this, that he lay down his life for his friends'* (John 15:13).

Jesus was a man of integrity, gentleness, humility, joy, peace and love.

His words were truthful and helpful

- Guards were sent to arrest Jesus. They returned without him and said, *'No one ever spoke the way this man does'* (John 7:46).
- After he had been teaching the crowds: *'All spoke well of him and were amazed at the gracious words that came from his lips'* (Luke 4:22).

People's sharp tongues and cruel comments can hurt, but Jesus used his words wisely to encourage or warn.

The apostle Paul describes a good character in this way: *'The fruit of the Spirit is love, joy, peace, patience, kindness, goodness, faithfulness, gentleness and self-control'* (Galatians 5:22,23). This is the best description of Jesus.

Jesus also spoke plainly and truthfully. He never covered up sin and he condemned hypocrisy and deceit and warned of hell for the unrepentant.

Two hundred years ago the French Emperor Napoleon fought and ruled with power and might. He said this about Jesus: *'I tell you that Jesus Christ is no mere man. Between him and every other person in the world there is no possible comparison. Alexander, Caesar, Charlemagne, and I have founded empires. But on what did we rest the creation of our genius? Upon force. Jesus Christ founded His empire upon love; and at this hour millions of men would die for Him'*— They have and they still do.

Napoleon admired Jesus for his power and authority—but without force

8. JESUS—his supremacy

Jesus is the supreme power and authority over all

Many people, in their need, seek help from a 'power' greater than themselves to bring them to a better life: departed loved ones, angels, religion, nature, the universe, energy, ego, even group meetings. The Bible tells us clearly that Jesus Christ is the highest power and authority of all. He has command over everything:

'The Son is the image of the invisible God, the firstborn over all creation. For by him all things were created: things in heaven and on earth, visible and invisible, whether thrones or powers or rulers or authorities; all things have been created through him and for him. He is before all things, and in him all things hold together' (Colossians 1:15–17).

Jesus demonstrated his authority over everything when he walked this earth. He took on and beat the three strongest things known to humanity: sin, demons and death.

Sin. Throughout his life on earth Jesus was tempted to sin, like we all are. One terrible episode is recorded in Matthew 4:1–11. Sin is a powerful master defeating the whole human race—but Jesus beat sin; he was *'tempted in every way, just as we are—yet was without sin'* (Hebrews 4:15).

Demons. The devil has control over unseen evil demons who spoil people's lives and mess up the world. On more than one occasion Jesus was confronted by demons ganging up against him. One time, he came across a man who was possessed by a whole legion of demons: *'This man lived in the tombs, and no one could bind him anymore, not even with a chain... Night and day among the tombs and in the hills he would cry out and cut himself with stones'* (Mark 5:3-5). Jesus rescued this man and freed him from his awful life by casting out all those demons. His was the greatest power.

Death. There is nothing stronger or more unavoidable than death. Death beats everyone. Death is a terrible thing separating a person from their loved ones. But Jesus beat death by raising others and then himself dying and rising never to die again. Jesus can now say *'I am the Living One; I was dead, and behold I am alive for ever and ever!'* (Revelation 1:18). So, the Christian can say, *'Where, O death, is your victory? Where, O death, is your sting?'* (1 Corinthians 15:55).

Those who follow Jesus have found the Highest Power that can ever be and ever will be.

Jesus came to set people free from whatever holds them in bondage

9. JESUS—the worker of miracles

The miracles of Jesus were to prove that he was who he claimed to be

Bible prophecies foretold that the Messiah would work wonders and people would be amazed: *'Then will the eyes of the blind be opened and the ears of the deaf unstopped. Then will the lame leap like a deer, and the mute tongue shout for joy.'* (Isaiah 35:5,6).

Jesus showed his power over nature: feeding more than five thousand people with five loaves and two fish (Mark 6), stilling a violent storm on a lake (Mark 4), walking on water (Mark 6)—and many more. However, most of his miracles were to help people: restoring sight to a blind man (Mark 8); curing the demon-possessed (Mark 5); healing a cripple (John 5); healing leprosy (Matthew 8); enabling a deaf and dumb person to hear and speak (Mark 7); and raising the dead (John 11).

The purpose of Jesus' miracles

Jesus didn't work his miracles to make money or to entertain people:

- They were signs to show that Jesus was who he claimed to be. Anyone could say 'I am the Messiah', but how can we tell if they are fake or lying? The miracles of Jesus proved who he was. No one has ever done miracles like his. His very first miracle *'revealed his glory, and his disciples put their faith in him'* (John 2:11).

In his Gospel, the apostle John included many miracles of Jesus and added, *'These are written that you may* believe that Jesus is the Christ, the Son of God, and that by believing you may have life in his name' (John 20:31).

- Jesus also worked his miracles to help people. The apostle Peter said that Jesus *'went around doing good and healing all who were under the power of the devil'* (Acts 10:38). He healed to show that he cared and that he had the power to do what no one else could do. His healing miracles were instant and complete.

- Jesus' miracles showed what the world should really be like. It should never have been like it is now. Rebellion against God spoiled it all. Jesus' miracles reversed the results of sin and gave a preview of what it will be like when God creates a new heaven and earth: *'He will wipe every tear from their eyes. There will be no more death or mourning or crying or pain, for the old order of things has passed away'* (Revelation 21:4).

'Jesus put his hands on the man's eyes. Then his eyes were opened, his sight was restored, and he saw everything clearly' (Mark 8:25)

10. JESUS—the Man of love

Jesus was a man of love who did good to all people and never hurt or injured anyone

Our world is screaming with violence and terrorism. Social media swarms with hatred, racism and slander. Anger boils over. Our streets, homes, schools and colleges live in fear of bullying and gang warfare. It is a dark and fearful world.

Jesus, the Man of Love, enters into this dark world lighting it up and filling the hearts of men and women with love rather than hate.

Jesus loved people

- Jesus often stayed with a family in Bethany. Mary and Martha were sisters, and when their brother Lazarus died, Jesus cried and the mourners said, *'See how he loved him'* (John 11:36).

- Jesus loved those who followed him and told them to do the same: *'Love one another, as I have loved you'* (John 13:34).

- Jesus even loved people who rejected him. A rich young man loved his money above everything and sadly walked away from Jesus, yet: *'Jesus looked at him and loved him'* (Mark 10:21).

People said all sorts of cruel things about Jesus, but no-one could say he didn't love people. He loved God and people perfectly.

Jesus' love for you

If you follow Jesus, you will experience a love that you cannot imagine, a love that is unconditional. You may think of yourself as rubbish and too bad to be loved. You may think your sin is deeper than the sea, but you need to know that Jesus' love goes deeper than your sin.

'Love is patient, love is kind. It does not envy, it does not boast, it is not proud. It is not rude, it is not self-seeking, it is not easily angered, it keeps no record of wrongs. Love does not delight in evil but rejoices with the truth. It always protects, always trusts, always hopes, always perseveres. Love never fails' (1 Corinthians 13:4–8).

This is a perfect description of Jesus.

The greatest way Jesus showed his love was giving himself on the cross to save a rebel world from sin and shame. He said, *'Greater love has no one than this, that he lay down his life for his friends'* (John 15:13). That is exactly what Jesus did.

What's more, he will fill your own heart and life with love: *'God has poured out his love into our hearts by the Holy Spirit, whom he has given us'* (Romans 5:5).

The love of Jesus in our lives brings a calm peace

11. JESUS — the Counsellor

We all need someone who will listen to us, understands us and knows just the right thing to say

An ancient Bible prophecy foretold that Jesus would be a *Wonderful Counsellor* (Isaiah 9:6). A **counsellor** listens to people, knows about people and how to help them in their life situations. A **wonderful** counsellor knows how to do this supremely well.

Jesus knows our inner need

Jesus knows everything about us. John, one of his disciples, states that Jesus: *'did not need man's testimony about man, for he knew what was in a man'* (John 2:25). He knows our ambitions, fears, dreams and our failures. He knows those dark secrets we keep to ourselves. He knows our confusion, self-doubt and our anxiety. He knows our deepest needs to be loved, known, understood, and valued. He sees behind the mask, behind the pretence, behind the tears and smiles. He knows the real you.

Jesus knows how to help

Jesus helped so many people in their need. He is able to help because he is God and because he lived a human life and *'shared in our humanity'* (Hebrews 2:14). He knows what it's like to live in a messed-up, broken world. Jesus didn't live in a palace far removed from human poverty; he didn't spend much time with people who 'held it all together' and proudly thought they didn't need help. He mixed with those who were at rock-bottom; with people who were broken, wounded and sinful.

Jesus knows what to do and say to help us. His words in the Bible are life-giving words. He can heal those wounds, shine light in those dark places and cast away those doubts and fears. He can give life purpose and meaning and set us free from sin, anguish, guilt, shame and self-doubt. Jesus helps us to be who God created us to be and to live the life that God intended us to live.

We can call on Jesus

Throughout history people have received his help when they have turned to him.

For all who call on Jesus, he is the Wonderful Counsellor

- *'I call on the LORD in my distress, and he answers me'* (Psalm 120:1).
- *'They cried to the LORD in their trouble, and he saved them from their distress'* (Psalm 107:13).
- A man cried out to Jesus: *'I do believe; help me overcome my unbelief'* (Mark 9:24) and Jesus answered his prayer.

But there is more we need to know about Jesus. Keep reading!

12. JESUS—the Saviour for all

No one has sunk so far that God cannot forgive them or is so 'good' that they do not need God to forgive them

Sin is a word not much used today, yet it is a horrible reality in all of us. The Bible reminds us: *'All have sinned and fall short of the glory of God'* (Romans 3:23).

In the Bible God tells us what is right and what is wrong; and in his life Jesus showed what a perfect life looks like. I sin when I put myself in the place of God and decide how I will live without any reference to God. I become self-righteous and self-sufficient, or full of self-pity and self-destruction. It's all about me and nothing about God.

All sin angers God and is against God, because it spoils the world he created. If you steal my phone, I can forgive you. But that sin was against God also and he needs to forgive you too.

Jesus came to forgive people their sins against God

Jesus spent so much time with 'sinners' that the proud religious people despised him and said, *'This man welcomes sinners and eats with them'* (Luke 15:2). This is exactly why he came to earth—to be a Saviour for sinners!

- Hypocrites were demanding that a woman be stoned to death because she was caught in an immoral sexual act. Jesus challenged them: *'If any one of you is without sin, let him be the first to throw a stone at her.'* No one could. So, Jesus said to the woman, *'Neither do I condemn you. Go now and leave your life of sin'* (John 8:7, 11).

- To a young man whose greatest need was forgiveness, Jesus said, *'Your sins are forgiven.'* The religious-types were outraged, *'Why does this fellow talk like that? He's blaspheming! Who can forgive sins but God alone?'* (Mark 2:6, 7). Jesus is God, so that's why he can forgive our sins if we turn to him.

- Seeing the repentance of Zacchaeus, a well-known cheat who had become rich at the expense of others, Jesus said, *'Today salvation has come to this house'*, and added, *'The Son of Man came to seek and to save what was lost'* (Luke 19:9, 10).

Forgiveness is one of the most beautiful words in our language—it leads to reconciliation, that is, putting a bad relationship right. We all, without exception, need it. When we turn to God in repentance and faith, we can know the peace and joy of sins forgiven and being reconciled to God—whoever we are and whatever we have done.

When Zacchaeus, a fraudster, became a disciple of Jesus, he gave back what he had stolen

13. JESUS—the Liberator

Jesus broke many of the social customs and religious traditions of his day. But he did so for very good reasons

Not once did Jesus do or say—or even think—anything wrong. He was perfect but not dull; humble but not boring. You never knew what he was going to do next. This made him unpredictable and thrilling— and for some, dangerous. He had everyone on edge. The authorities closely watched his every move to find something wrong with him. He once challenged the leaders: *'Can any of you prove me guilty of sin?'* (John 8:46) — but they couldn't answer!

Jesus challenged tradition

Jesus lived at a time and in a place where the authorities insisted on people doing things according to their tradition. There was much prejudice and oppression, and women were generally at the bottom of the social pile. Jesus rebelled against all this and was counter-cultural, turning the world's thinking on its head. Jesus came to show what the kingdom of God looks like—when we obey God's rules.

Jesus challenged the man-made cultural and religious rules of his day. He insisted that people were more important than rules. He claimed that the condition of the inner life, the heart, was far more important than rules about outward observance and ritual.

Jesus set people free

Against society's rules, he touched those with contagious diseases and spent time teaching women. He loved the weak, vulnerable, voiceless, unworthy, dirty, outcast people in this world and showed them compassion, justice and mercy. This is what the true kingdom of God looks like. Not proud, self-satisfied, social and religious intolerance.

Jesus still cares!

Jesus holds the good of humanity in his heart. His opposition to intolerance, bigotry and extremism was for the cause of love. He wants people to be set free from cultural and religious laws that do not come from God. He wants people to love God and love their neighbours. He wants all of us to live in the freedom that God's true law can give—a freedom that enables people to enjoy a full and 'clean' life.

All this showed his love for God and his perfect law that gives freedom. It also showed his love for people and their dignity and value.

Against society's rules, Jesus touched lepers who were despised as 'unclean'

14. JESUS—the Teacher of truth

Jesus is the greatest teacher the world has known. For two thousand years untold billions have been living by what he said

We are flooded with other people's opinions and advice today. Through social media anyone and everyone can let the world know what they think. Most will soon be forgotten.

Jesus the teacher

Jesus spent so much of his time teaching, and because of who he is his words were real truth. He didn't offer ideas or suggestions, he spoke *'the words of God'* (John 3:34). He alone has *'the words of eternal life'* (John 6:68).

Jesus told people what God is like and how they could be delivered from sin. He spoke as one who had the right to tell people what to do, how to live, how to make the world a better place and how to get safely to heaven. His messages were so powerful that *'The crowds were amazed at his teaching, because he taught as one who had authority, and not as their teachers of the law'* (Matthew 7:28,29).

Jesus said it first

Many of Jesus' sayings are still in common use today:

- *'Turn the other cheek'* (Matthew 5:39)
- *'Go the extra mile'* (Matthew 5:41)
- *'Love your enemies'* (Matthew 5:44)
- *'Do to others what you would have them do to you'* (Matthew 7:12)

And there are many more!

The importance of practice

Thousands heard Jesus' teaching, but many ignored it. It is not hearing his words that makes the difference, but putting them into practice. Jesus told a story to illustrate the vital importance of doing what he said:

'Everyone who hears these words of mine and puts them into practice is like a wise man who built his house on the rock. The rain came down, the streams rose, and the winds blew and beat against that house; yet it did not fall, because it had its foundation on the rock. But everyone who hears these words of mine and does not put them into practice is like a foolish man who built his house on sand. The rain came down, the streams rose, and the winds blew and beat against that house, and it fell with a great crash' (Matthew 7:24-27).

When the storms of life hit, will your life stand or crash? Is your life built on the solid foundation of faith in Jesus and obedience to his word, the Bible?

Jesus warned that unless our life is built on his teaching, it would collapse around us

15. JESUS—
the Victim with a purpose

Crucifixion was so agonizingly cruel and humiliating that the Romans never crucified a woman or a Roman citizen

Jesus would have suffered terribly. He was crucified outside Jerusalem at 9.00 in the morning on a hill called Golgotha, which means 'place of a skull'.

He was stripped, beaten mercilessly, mocked and jeered by all who gathered at the ugly scene of public execution. His feet were nailed to the upright beam and his hands to the crossbeam. There was no protection from the scorching sun and his thirst was intense. Breathing eventually became impossible and the prisoner normally died of suffocation. Jesus died at 3.00 in the afternoon and was certified dead by a Roman centurion and his four infantrymen (Mark 15:44, 45).

The human reason for his death

Religion and politics were to blame. The religious leaders hated Jesus and invented charges of treason against Rome. Pilate, the Roman Governor in Jerusalem, was frightened by their threats, and was afraid of consequences in Rome if he let Jesus go. So, Jesus was handed over to be crucified.

The real reason for his death

However, there was a much deeper meaning to the death of Jesus. Throughout the Jewish Scriptures—our Old

Testament—the death of the Messiah had been predicted. For example, one thousand years before the cross: *'All who see me mock me; they hurl insults, shaking their heads: "He trusts in the LORD; let the LORD rescue him. Let him deliver him, since he delights in him."'* (Psalm 22:7, 8). Read chapter 20 of this booklet and you will see that is exactly what happened. (Also look up Matthew 27:41–43.)

Then, seven hundred years before the cross: *'He was pierced for our transgressions, he was crushed for our iniquities; the punishment that brought us peace was on him...'* (Isaiah 53:5).

The cross is the place where Jesus took the punishment for the sins of all who trust him, and the just anger of God against our sin is turned away. But why such a *terrible* death? It helps us see what a terrible mess sin makes of life.

The amazing message

Jesus' death means that when we trust in him our sins are forgiven immediately and God's anger will not crush us on the Judgment Day: *'Whoever believes in the Son has eternal life, but whoever rejects the Son will not see life, for God's wrath remains on him'* (John 3:36).

'He himself bore our sins in his body on the cross...' (1 Peter 2:22)

16. JESUS—
the undefeated Victor

The resurrection of Jesus Christ from the dead is absolutely central to Christian faith and essential for Christian life

After Jesus' crucifixion his disciples thought it was all over. But it was far from over. Jesus, the *'author of life'* (Acts 3:15) came back from the dead on the third day. He won the greatest fight of history—Jesus defeated death. He claimed, *'I am the Resurrection and the Life'* (John 11:25) and he proved it.

Back to life?

Jesus did not merely revive in the tomb to come back to the same life and existence as before.

- It was not reincarnation. He did not come back as another being to live on earth and die again.

A tomb in Jerusalem, similar to that in which Jesus' body was laid

- It was not make-believe. The disciples did not imagine it. Crowds don't have hallucinations.

- Jesus did not simply live on in the spirit of his disciples just as a celebrity 'lives on' in the spirit of their fans.

- It was not a conjuring trick with bones. The disciples were not fools or liars.

Jesus' resurrection was his real physical body—a body that could be touched and could walk and talk (Luke 24:15–17). It was a body that would never die again because it was imperishable and immortal (1 Corinthians 15:53, 54).

His disciples saw him

Over forty days Jesus appeared to his disciples on at least eleven occasions in different places. He *gave them many convincing proofs that he was alive* (Acts 1:3). They were so convinced of his resurrection that they were prepared to suffer torture and death for him.

What the resurrection of Jesus means

Jesus' resurrection transformed his disciples. Their misery turned to joy, their hopelessness turned to assurance, and their fear turned to courage. If Jesus did not rise then everything he said and claimed is a lie and, as the apostle Paul wrote, Christians *are to be pitied more than all* (1 Corinthians 15:19).

For Christians, life and eternity now look very different because of Jesus' resurrection. His resurrection guarantees the resurrection of all who trust him. Jesus said, *'Because I live you also will live'* (John 14:19).

We suggest you read the booklet in this series: *Is it True? The resurrection of Jesus.* Turn to page 44 for details.

17. JESUS— the unavoidable Judge

The night before his crucifixion, Jesus told his disciples that he would die, rise again and return to heaven to prepare a place for them

This was his promise: *'If I go and prepare a place for you, I will come back and take you to be with me that you also may be where I am'* (John 14:3). He has given his promise and now we wait for his return to earth. But with the promise is a warning.

What will he do when he returns?

The apostle Paul told philosophers in Athens that God *'has set a day when he will judge the world with justice by the man he has appointed'* (Acts 17:31). So, a judgement day is set. Jesus has been appointed as Judge. Everyone wants justice and Jesus will judge fairly. On that final day, justice will be done. No one will avoid it.

What will happen?

Here is the description that Jesus himself gave: *'All the nations will be gathered before him, and he will separate*

There is no appeal beyond the Supreme Court in London. It is the ultimate court of the land

the people one from another as a shepherd separates the sheep from the goats' (Matthew 25:32).

But how do we know if we have done enough good things that will stand up to God's judgement on that day? The simple fact is that not one of us has. And that is exactly why Jesus had to die in the place of all who will trust him and become his followers. *'He who conceals his sins does not prosper, but whoever confesses and renounces them finds mercy'* (Proverbs 28:13).

On that day there will be a final division between those who have trusted Jesus as their Saviour and those who have not. Jesus will make no mistakes. Those who have trusted Jesus will be welcomed into God's everlasting kingdom.

But those who have rejected him in this life will take that tragic decision into eternity. Jesus will say to them: *'Depart from me … into the eternal fire prepared for the devil and his angels'* (Matthew 25:41). This will be terrible—more than words can describe.

When will he return?

We don't know when. But Jesus warned his disciples to be ready at any time (Matthew 24:36).

How can I be ready? *'If you confess with your mouth, "Jesus is Lord," and believe in your heart that God raised him from the dead, you will be saved'* (Romans 10:9).

Are you ready right now to meet Jesus, the Judge, as your Saviour?

18. JESUS—the disciple-maker

You have been introduced to Jesus. You have seen that he is the greatest person who has ever lived, the highest Authority there will ever be and the only Saviour from sin

Jesus called all sorts of people to be his disciples and to follow him. From fishermen to accountants, from the poor to the very rich. He commanded each of them: *'Follow me'*.

Now Jesus calls you. Although salvation is a free gift, true discipleship can be costly: *'If anyone would come after me, he must deny himself and take up his cross and follow me'* (Mark 8:34).

What does it mean to follow Jesus?

- It means beginning to **trust** him by receiving **Jesus as your Saviour**. *'To all who received him, to those who believed in his name, he gave the right to become children of God'* (John 1:12).

- It means beginning to **obey** him by receiving **Jesus as your King**. You change your mind about the way you have been living--putting yourself first in place of God. You now begin to live under God's kind rule.

- It means beginning to **believe** the things he taught by receiving **Jesus as your Teacher**. He taught us what to believe about God and the right way to live: *'If you love me, you will obey what I command'* (John 14:15).

- It means beginning to **behave** with **Jesus as your Example**. *'To this you were called, because Christ suffered for you, leaving you an example, that you* *should follow in his steps'* (1 Peter 2:21). You begin to live a worthwhile life as it should be lived.

That journey starts when you tell God you have rebelled against him and you want to be forgiven and change your direction—that's called repentance.

We suggest you go back and read again chapter 15 'Jesus—The victim with a purpose'.

God the Holy Spirit will come into your life— silently and invisibly—to help you to live as a Christian (John 14:16, 23 ,25).

This does not mean that all your problems are solved, or that you will have no more tears, sickness or trials. But it does mean your sins will be forgiven and that God will be your Father and Jesus your Friend for ever.

> *'Salvation is found in no one else, for there is no other name under heaven given to mankind by which we must be saved'* (Acts 4:12)

The first disciples of Jesus were ordinary, everyday people

19. JESUS—
the builder of his Church

Jesus promised, *'I will build my church, and the gates of Hades (Hell) will not overcome it'* (Matthew 16:18)

By the word 'church', Jesus was not talking about buildings or denominations, but about people. The church is made up of people from all over the world who follow Jesus. Jesus promises that his church (his people) will never be overpowered by death or evil: *'Christ loved the church and gave himself up for her, to make her holy… and to present her to himself as a radiant church… holy and blameless'* (Ephesians 5:25–27).

More than this, he has promised a wonderful eternal future in God's kingdom: *'He will wipe every tear from their eyes. There will be no more death or mourning or crying or pain, for the old order of things has passed away'* (Revelation 21:3–4).

It is a great privilege to belong to his church.

After Jesus' resurrection in Jerusalem three thousand people started following Jesus—they were the first church. They were baptised and *'They devoted themselves to the apostles' teaching and to the fellowship, to the breaking of bread and to prayer'* (Acts 2:42). This verse sums up the true church:

- **The apostles' teaching:** This is Bible teaching to help us grow in our understanding of God and the Christian life.

- **Fellowship:** This is meeting together to encourage and support each other in both joy and sadness.

- **Breaking of bread:** This is the Lord's Supper (or communion) where Christians remember the death and resurrection of Jesus.
- **Prayer:** This is when the church meets to bring their thankfulness, worship and requests to God.

No matter how long someone has been following Jesus they still need the church to help them survive and thrive in living for Jesus.

The church is called the *'body of Christ'* (1 Corinthians 12:27). When Jesus lived on earth, he did so much good: he fed the hungry, helped the poor, repaired peoples' lives and proclaimed the good news of salvation. Jesus is still doing the same things today through the church. The church is a great benefit in this sinful, broken and sad world.

If you are a Christian or want to know more, find a church that preaches the Bible, cares for all people—including the poor, the vulnerable and the abused—and reaches others with the good news of salvation. And if you are not a Christian, why not put your trust in him now?

Jesus is the builder of his church

20. The account of Jesus' death and resurrection from Luke's Gospel

Luke 23:32–47

Two other men, both criminals, were also led out with him to be executed. When they came to the place called the Skull, there they crucified him, along with the criminals—one on his right, the other on his left. Jesus said, "Father, forgive them, for they do not know what they are doing." And they divided up his clothes by casting lots.

The people stood watching, and the rulers even sneered at him. They said, "He saved others; let him save himself if he is the Christ of God, the Chosen One."

The soldiers also came up and mocked him. They offered him wine vinegar and said, "If you are the king of the Jews, save yourself."

There was a written notice above him, which read: THIS IS THE KING OF THE JEWS.

One of the criminals who hung there hurled insults at him: "Aren't you the Christ? Save yourself and us!"

But the other criminal rebuked him. "Don't you fear God," he said, "since you are under the same sentence? We are punished justly, for we are getting what our deeds deserve. But this man has done nothing wrong."

Then he said, "Jesus, remember me when you come into your kingdom."

Jesus answered him, "I tell you the truth, today you will be with me in paradise."

It was now about the sixth hour, and darkness came over the whole land until the ninth hour, for the sun stopped shining. And the curtain of the temple was torn in two. Jesus called out with a loud voice, "Father, into your hands I commit my spirit." When he had said this, he breathed his last.

The centurion, seeing what had happened, praised God and said, "Surely this was a righteous man."

Luke 24:1–8

On the first day of the week, very early in the morning, the women took the spices they had prepared and went to the tomb. They found the stone rolled away from the tomb, but when they entered, they did not find the body of the Lord Jesus. While they were wondering about this, suddenly two men in clothes that gleamed like lightning stood beside them.

In their fright the women bowed down with their faces to the ground, but the men said to them, "Why do you look for the living among the dead? He is not here; he has risen! Remember how he told you, while he was still with you in Galilee: 'The Son of Man must be delivered into the hands of sinful men, be crucified and on the third day be raised again.'"

Then they remembered his words.

The following three booklets, just like this one, introduce the truth about the Christian faith

IS IT TRUE?
Evidence for the Bible

Clive Anderson and Brian Edwards

Too often people dismiss the Bible as unreliable without realising that archaeologists have uncovered so much that proves its accuracy. The Bible is full of people, places and

events that are set in real points of history; it is easy to check it out and discover just how reliable it is.

This booklet introduces you to a few examples of the irrefutable evidence demonstrating that the Bible is a book of accurate and reliable history.

Obtainable at www.dayone.co.uk
ISBN 978-1-84625-502-1 | REF IIT5021

IS IT TRUE? Evidence for Creation

Professors Stuart Burgess and Andy McIntosh ed. Brian Edwards

Did the precise movements of the planets, the regular seasons of the year, the reliance of all living things upon each other and the awesome detail of life, result from a series of unimaginable probabilities — or does such complex design point to a wise and powerful Creator?

Here, in brief, is the evidence of 'irreducible complexity' illustrated by two top scientists. Enjoy the panorama of a creation so beautifully detailed, ordered and complex that it would be unbelievable if it was not there in front of us.

Obtainable at www.dayone.co.uk
ISBN 978-1-84625-609-7 | REF IITC6097

Please see next page for *IS IT TRUE? The resurrection of Jesus*

IS IT TRUE?
The resurrection of Jesus

Brian H Edwards

The fact that Jesus Christ lived in Judea and was crucified in AD 33 is undeniably supported by history. It is also a matter of history that all his disciples believed that Jesus had risen from the dead and they had personally seen him.

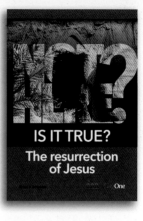

But did he really rise?

If the resurrection of Jesus is true, then it is the most astounding and significant miracle ever recorded in the history of the human race. Here, in this booklet, is the evidence for that miracle.

To ignore the implications of Jesus' resurrection is the gravest mistake anyone can make.

Obtainable at www.dayone.co.uk
ISBN 978-1-84625-626-4 | REF IITR6264

IS IT TRUE?
Who Is Jesus?

No one in history has lived such a perfect, beautiful and significant life as Jesus Christ. His life, death, resurrection and his teaching have changed the story of our world.

Tragically, the Western world has side-lined Jesus today and most people have little knowledge of who he is and what he accomplished. The result is a society sinking into violence and moral decay.

People are fed with false ideas of Jesus that have nothing to do with either the Bible or historical fact. The evidence for the historical Jesus and his resurrection is strong. See the booklet in this series *Is it True? The resurrection of Jesus.*

This booklet, *Who is Jesus?*, introduces the real Jesus: who he is, what he is like, all that he accomplished and how you can know him for yourself. Here you will discover the glory of his person and the pure dignity of his character.

Joint publication with Christian Prison Resourcing and Day One

Day One Publications
Ryelands Road Leominster HR6 8NZ
Email: sales@dayone.co.uk
www.dayone.co.uk
☏ +44 (0) 1568 613 740
☏ Toll Free 888 329 6630 (North America)

Christian Prison Resourcing
PO Box 61685
London SE9 9BL
www.cprministries.org.uk

ISBN 978-1-84625-666-0